Kenneth Hellawell

Best wishes from Peter Iveffren

a signed edition from

GREAT NORTHERN

LEEDS
CHANGING PLACES

PETER TUFFREY

GREAT N-ORTHERN

ACKNOWLEDGEMENTS

I am grateful for the assistance received from the following people:
David Clay, Norman Ellis, Stuart Hastings, Peter Jary, Paul License, Hugh Parkin, Jane Salt.
Special thanks to my son Tristram Tuffrey for general support and encouragement.

Great Northern Books
PO Box 1380, Bradford, BD5 5FB
www.greatnorthernbooks.co.uk

ISBN: 978-1-912101-64-1

Design and layout: David Burrill

CIP Data
A catalogue for this book is available from the British Library

Printed & bound in India

INTRODUCTION

When producing a book of this type careful planning has to take place. There has to be a fine balance of old, barely recognisable views, positioned above modern ones which still retain a fragment of the older scene, yet show vast changes. This has been uppermost in my mind when compiling *Leeds Changing Places* as the city, like countless others throughout the country, has witnessed significant alterations from the early 19th century.

A few of the book's old pictures stretch back to just after the mid-19th century and feature the work of Leeds photographer, Edmund Wormald. Setting up his own photographic studio in Wellington Street, Leeds in 1860, Edmund, who was later joined by his brother Joseph, used the photographic medium to record many Leeds buildings and local street scenes.

These include views of Boar Lane before widening; the buildings removed for the building of the ambitious County Arcade; the 16th century timber-framed buildings on the west side of Briggate; and the remarkable view of the City Square/Wellington Street/Park Row junction before the area was remodelled.

The mid-19th century in Leeds was a period when Hull-born architect Cuthbert Brodrick produced drawings for a number of the town's most recognisable buildings: the Town Hall; Mechanics Institute (now Leeds Museum); the Corn Exchange; not forgetting the small group of shops on Calverley Street. Thankfully, although many are not operating under their original purpose, the buildings thrive today, having been cleaned and are currently, and rightly, protected under Listed status.

For much of the 19th century, Leeds' prosperity was reflected via the splendidly designed commercial and business premises along the various thoroughfares such as Park Row, Boar Lane, Commercial Street, Vicar Lane and Briggate. They were the work of quite a number of extremely competent architects including George Corson, Thomas Ambler and Percy Robinson, to mention just a few.

Sadly, some of the buildings have been lost or others disfigured in the various large scale developments or even smaller alterations that have occurred.

Good examples of large scale destruction are visible along Bond Street and Lands Lane. In the latter area we realise it is a great pity the Victoria Arcade was lost in the later development of the entire Schofield's site. Smaller examples of loss through commercial fads are witnessed in Commercial Street where George Corson's frontage on the Harvey, Reynolds & Co. building has been ruined by the ground floor alterations.

The turn of the 19th century saw commercial building reach a peak with a small number of arcades constructed, in particular, the County Arcade, the entire complex, including the Empire Palace Theatre, designed by Frank Matcham. Whilst the theatre has been lost the area has been developed further and falls under the umbrella of the Victoria Quarter.

Into the 20th century, and one of the first major developments was the construction of a new Market Hall. Externally, it may not have altered much over the years, apart from the insertion of the Vicar Lane entrance, but has overcome fires and still makes a valuable contribution to the city's commerce and is popular with shoppers. As will be seen in this book some of the external ground floor shop frontages have not altered noticeably over the years and so do not detract from the building as a whole.

With the build up of motorised traffic during the first few decades of the century, it was essential that the Headrow should be widened to facilitate east–west movement through the city. Pictures are included of various stretches to show what was lost in the setting back of the street line, all adhering to the grand plan produced by architect Reginald Blomfield.

Housing was also a pressing problem during the early 20th century and ultimately resulted in the construction of the sprawling Quarry Hill flats. At one time they presented a spectacular sight from a number of viewpoints within the city, but became a spectacular failure and eyesore and were demolished, after a relatively short life-span, during the late 1970s. Nonetheless, an area of the vacant site was put to good use with the construction of the West Yorkshire Playhouse.

One of the post-War problems confronting Leeds was the movement of traffic around the city and this saw the development of the Inner Relief Road, work starting in 1964. Included in the book are pictures taking place on the Westgate tunnel and the Regent Street vicinity.

An area designated in the city's 1951 Development Plan as a multi-storey car park and bus station became, during the early 1960s, the Merrion Centre, then the largest indoor shopping centre in the UK. Illustrations in this book show the centre under construction. Having undergone a number of redevelopments over the years, the Merrion Centre is still a lively area.

At the time of writing, large and small building projects continue in the city. A very ambitious scheme along Eastgate, and to the rear of Vicar Lane, will see Victoria Gate emerge whilst an example of a smaller scale development is the hotel being constructed on the corner of Woodhouse Lane/Calverley Street.

Finally, and perhaps not before time, one of the oldest areas of Leeds, Lower Kirkgate, neglected for quite a considerable number of years, became the subject of a recent Leeds Council Planning Statement. Hopefully this will see a sensitive regeneration of the area which can trace its history to at least the Anglo-Saxon period.

ALBION STREET/BOND STREET CORNER

A once familiar facade in the centre of the top picture is the *Yorkshire Post* office at no 55. But, the main interest is perhaps the classical, gabled building on the far right. Formerly housed there was a branch of the Bank of England and also the Leeds Stock Exchange. In later years it was partly tenanted by solicitors Ford & Warren. The building was demolished for West Riding House to be constructed on the site following a compulsory purchase order in 1968. Existing on the corner from 1931, the *Yorkshire Post* moved to new premises on the former site of Bean Ing Mill, Wellington Street, in 1970.

BISHOPGATE STREET

Bishopgate Street facing south-east, with Mill Hill in the distance on the left, and Neville Street to the right. Bishopgate still makes an important contribution to assist the flow of traffic in this tricky city bottleneck today as it did when the top picture was taken in 1969. The city station signal box under wraps to the right no longer controls movement in the station area, as that is presently controlled from York. Use is still made of the commercial premises beneath the arches and newspapers are still available but presently on sale in a different location than before. The towering car park at the rear dates from c. 1992. Bright colours on the bridges, shop facias and signage and street furniture bring much-needed relief to a once drab area of the city.

BISHOPGATE STREET

Above, the original Queen's Hotel (right) is viewed from Bishopgate Street looking south-west during the mid-1930s with the railway bridge on the extreme left. The Queen's Hotel was actually built over a river. This was the 'Goit', a tributary of the River Aire, and this added to the difficulties of the builders Wm Nicholson & Son. The hotel was said to be 'of a very ornate character, in the Italian style of architecture.' It was also noted for its dining room lined in Burmantofts faience. The wisdom of the Midland Railway Co's decision to build a hotel in Leeds was soon apparent, for in 1867 a new wing was added, and in 1898 still another wing was necessary. The extensions were designed by Midland Railway architect C. T. Trubshaw, and Wm. Nicholson & Son, once more, carried out the construction work. The entire structure was demolished in the mid-1930s for the building of a new hotel.

BOAR LANE/PARK ROW/BISHOPGATE STREET JUNCTION

The view is from the City Square looking to the Boar Lane/Park Row/Bishopgate Street junction, where it is evident that motor buses have replaced electric trams. The city adopted horse-drawn trams (September 16, 1871 to October 13, 1901), steam trams (June 17, 1880 to April 1, 1902) and electric trams (July, 28 1897 to November 7, 1959). The building on the right, designed by W.W. Gwyther, was erected as the headquarters of the Yorkshire Banking Company in 1899 but has been converted to a nightclub. The Royal Exchange structure seen on the left in the top picture was erected between 1872 and 1875, but has been replaced by the Park Plaza Hotel.

BOAR LANE LOOKING EAST TO THE CORN EXCHANGE

Blackened over decades by the city's soot, many of the older buildings now present a cleaner countenance to Boar Lane – once the home of Leeds' most stylish shops – in a view looking east to the Corn Exchange. Much of the property on the south side was erected as part of the Boar Lane widening scheme of the late 1860s. Quite prominent in the top picture is Mark House incorporating the Grand Cafe/Restaurant and Dunn & Co, hatmakers on the corner with Alfred Street. Also visible is White Horse Restaurant, one of five city centre restaurants owned and run by the Fairburn family, at the Gascoigne Street corner. Unimaginable in times past, but quite common and most useful today is the box junction marked on the road. Once busy with motor transport, Boar Lane now has restricted vehicular access.

BOAR LANE, LOOKING WEST TO CITY SQUARE

Trams, horses and carts and motor vehicles vie for space and movement on Boar Lane in the old view but a kind of order is present in the modern one. Restricted parking is noted by yellow lines, spaces are marked for public transport (and shelters provided for the convenience of passengers), colour lights allow or restrict movement and bins are provided for litter. Many of the buildings have survived the test of time. Some have been restored sympathetically whilst on some sites there has been insensitive redevelopment. Overall the thoroughfare contributes much to the Leeds City Centre Conservation Area with many buildings having Listed status.

BOAR LANE, R. BOSTON & SONS

Richard Boston's premises were part of a large building erected on the south side of Boar Lane in the 1860s to the designs of architect Thomas Ambler. Boston (1843-1908) was one of a breed of 19th century shopkeepers who were prominent in local affairs, the like of which are not often seen today. He was a member of Leeds Council for twelve years and an elected member for the Headingley Ward in 1891. As chairman of the planning and property committee he bought six new parks for Leeds. His Boar Lane store was described in Waddington's 1894 *Guide to Leeds* as providing fifty varieties of fish including oysters, every bird imaginable, thirty six varieties of vegetables, and one hundred sorts of fruit.

BOAR LANE/NEW STATION STREET CORNER, WIGFALLS STORE

Wigfall's store offering furniture, radios and televisions is seen above at the Boar Lane/New Station Street corner in March 1973. The company once had other stores on Lower Briggate (electrical); Leeds Bridge (furniture) and Vicar Lane (clothing). Henry Wigfall established the firm in Sheffield around 1896 and during the 20th century it developed into a large concern with over 140 stores nationwide. The company was taken over by the Dixons chain in 1988. Wigfall's former store is presently occupied by another old company, Yates's – founded as Yates Wine Lodge in Oldham by Peter and Simon Yates during 1884. Despite a number of takeovers the name is still strong today.

BOAR LANE AT THE JUNCTION WITH LOWER BRIGGATE, FROM DUNCAN STREET

Edward Wormald, of 46 Great George Street, Leeds took the top picture around 1867. It shows the south side of Boar Lane before demolition during 1867-9 to facilitate widening from 21 feet to 66 feet. A road sign to the right warns the public not to venture through the area whilst the work is taking place. Traders' premises visible in Lower Briggate include those belonging to J.T. Beer (tailor) and Richard Fenton (hosier). Trevelyan Chambers, designed by Thomas Ambler and presently Listed, was subsequently built at the Briggate/Boar Lane junction on the set back street line. Occupied by a number of traders over the years, the building was renovated during the 1990s and is presently occupied by a hotel and a number of traders.

BOAR LANE FROM DUNCAN STREET LOOKING WEST

Gone are the top-covered, vestibuled electric trams and some of the once familiar traders along Boar Lane, but standing as prominent as ever – and cleaner – is Holy Trinity Church. Built in the late English renaissance style between 1722-7, the church was designed by William Etty of York. Besides still being very active within the city centre, promoting the heritage of building and its surroundings, Holy Trinity has also developed as a venue capable of hosting a broad range of arts events and corporate activities. The Holy Trinity website states: 'At our heart is the worshipping community of Holy Trinity Church and this engages two churches who use the building on a Sunday and offer Eucharistic services during the week.' Rising to 180 feet, the present steeple dates from 1839, when it replaced a wooden structure.

BOND STREET, FACING NORTH WEST

Bond Street once contained many of the city's impressive Victorian buildings and noted businesses belonging to: Powolny's Restaurant; Madame Louise, milliner; Johnson Brothers, dyers and dry cleaners; Dollond and Aitchison opticians; Berry's jewellers; and Pearson & Denham, photographic material dealers. The *Yorkshire Post Newspaper* occupied the building at the Bond Street/Albion Street corner between 1931-1970. The view along Bond Street changed, some will argue for the better, others for the worse, with the building of the Bond Street Shopping Centre (renamed Leeds Shopping Plaza in 1996 after restoration). Work was begun by John Brunton & Partners in 1974 and the Centre opened in 1977.

BRIDGE END, LOOKING NORTH

Bridge End is depicted looking north, from Meadow Lane, to the bridge over the River Aire, with Dock Street extending off to the right. The property, off centre to the right at the corner with Dock Street, was formerly a butcher's shop occupied by Frank Ambler. Further along to the left was Charles Best & Son, mill furnishers, and J. Lax & Son, leather merchants. This area underwent redevelopment in 1906 with the building of the Aire & Calder Navigation's offices on the Dock Street/Bridge End corner. Later, the premises were occupied by British Waterways. On this side of the thoroughfare, only the four-storey premises situated just south of Leeds Bridge, once tenanted by Hick Bros, ironmongers and tinners, are extant in this stretch today.

BRIDGE END LOOKING EAST

From the warehouses and factories on each side of the River Aire, in this view facing east from Leeds Bridge, many goods and materials were transported to and from the city. With the decline of waterways traffic many buildings have changed use over the years or have been demolished. The Leeds Waterfront was rejuvenated following the introduction of a Leeds City Council plan in the 1980s. Grants were made available to potential investors, and partnerships between the public and private sectors were established. Thereafter, old buildings were renovated and conserved and new ones added on derelict sites. Smart riverside and loft apartments, for city living, were created along with a number of shops, hotels, restaurants and bars.

BRIDGE END/SWINEGATE CORNER

The old view of the Briggate/Swinegate corner was taken just before the premises of piano and organ dealer Chas J. Fox were demolished and the street line set back. The Leeds Tramway headquarters were built on the remaining portion of land in 1915. During 1999 the building was converted into the Malmaison Hotel.

BRIGGATE (LOWER)

Lower Briggate is shown looking north from the junction with Call Lane (right) and Swinegate (left). One open-top tram in the top picture, no 149, has its route indicator displaying Hunslet. From March 1874, a horse car service operated between the city and Thwaite Gate (Crooked Billet). Then, from August 24, 1900 the line was electrified. Car no 64 is working on the Elland Road service. Charlotte Bronte once stayed at the Old George Hotel on the right. Dating from the 17th century, the premises were known under several names: Ye Bush, The George, Simpsons Commercial, and Old George Hotel before closure c. 1919. All the properties on the right were demolished during the 1930s and the area redeveloped. Note the fine array of signals fixed to the gantry, on the left, in the top picture.

BRIGGATE (LOWER)

An interesting group of 16th century, timber framed buildings, on the west side of Briggate, has been captured in the top picture by photographer Wormald during the 1860s. The buildings include, from l to r: wine and spirit merchant, Anthony Pickard; tobacconist, Miss Julia Picard; linen draper, Daniel Pickard & Co. Taking up much of the modern picture is Dyson's Chambers which replaced the Eagle Star Insurance property.

BRIGGATE (LOWER)

Shown, is the junction with Boar Lane and Duncan Street. In the old picture a malaise on the street is being caused by pedestrians, bicycles, trams, and motor vehicles all hustling for space. In the modern picture some might argue this has been alleviated to some extent with the help of traffic lights, road signage and markings – not to mention the absence of horses! Relocating from the Calls to this area, which was redeveloped c. 1865, was John Dyson & Sons, cloth-makers, diamond merchants, silversmiths and jewellers. Converting two cottages, 126/127 Briggate, Dyson established the firm in 1865. The large clock was installed around the same time with the smaller one being added in 1910 to celebrate the birthday of John Dyson's wife. Rebuilt and refurbished in 1980, the shop – the Time Ball Buildings – closed ten years later.

BRIGGATE WITH POLICEMAN ON TRAFFIC DUTY

Briggate came into being during 1207 when the road led to the north side of Leeds Bridge. In fact 'Briggate' means 'the road to the bridge.' For many years it provided one of the main routes north-south through the city and was frequented by many forms of transport. Thus, at one period, policemen were required on duty to assist with a coherent flow of traffic. From 1993 only public transport vehicles were allowed along the thoroughfare but three years later it was closed to all traffic. Between 2004 to 2006, Briggate was paved with York Stone. This has gone some way to make the street become more popular than ever especially with the redevelopment of many of the arcades along the route.

BRIGGATE/ALBION PLACE JUNCTION LOOKING WEST

Albion Place was extended from Briggate to Lands Lane in 1904 thus creating a new street. This involved the demolition of four properties along the west side of Briggate and two yards to the rear. Buildings recognisable in the top picture, dating from October 1902, include those belonging to, from l to r: the William IV Yard and pub; Miss J.A. Greetham's tea rooms; Renders' corset shop; W. Elliott's music shop; the Wheatsheaf Yard; Wheatsheaf pub; and Leopard Hotel. The new premises at the Albion Place/Briggate corner – nos 13 and 14 Albion Place – were designed by Percy Robinson in 1903. They were built for Eveleigh Bishop who was a stationer, printer, fancy goods importer, jeweller and silversmith. The premises comprise eight bays along Albion Place, a corner bay and a single bay on Briggate. The building was erected in a mixture of material: stone, red brick, buff, white and green faience.

BRIGGATE, QUEEN'S ARCADE

The Rose & Crown Yard, seen to the right in the top picture by Wormald, was transformed, c. 1889, into the Queen's Arcade, running between the west side of Briggate and Lands Lane. Within the old Yard, along with a collection of tradesmen and old shops, was the Rose & Crown public house – a coaching inn – also known as Binks' Hotel after one time landlady, Maria Binks. Traders identified on the Briggate frontage include: Ellen Barrows, boot and shoe dealer; J. & J.B. Bilbrough, chemist and druggist; and John W. Foster's trimming warehouse. London architect Edward Clark was responsible for designing the Arcade which was named in honour of Queen Victoria's Golden Jubilee. Built by Armistead & Proctor, the arcade when opened was described by the *Yorkshire Post* as 'light, bright and architecturally elegant, and is moreover, admirably designed from the business point of view.'

The Arcade underwent restoration in 1993, the work including the laying of a mosaic floor.

BRIGGATE, THE COUNTY ARCADE

During the late 19th century, further retail opportunities were provided by clearing old yards and creating continuous rows of shops in ornate, glass-roofed arcades. Properties in the above photograph, captured by Wormald in 1888, include nos 98 and 99, occupied by Smith Brothers, general and fancy drapers. These were taken, along with the White Hart Yard, in the County Arcade development. The Bay Horse pub closed not long after the Arcade was opened and a plaque still exists (bottom left in the modern picture) above the entrance to the Bay Horse Yard, stating: 'Bay Horse Hotel – Molineaux' – the latter being the surname of a former pub licensee.

BRIGGATE, COUNTY ARCADE

The County Arcade was designed by Frank Matcham who was also responsible for the Empire Palace Theatre in Briggate. Work started on the Arcade in 1898 and was part of the Leeds Estates Company redevelopment of Briggate. A central dome was decorated with figures representing Liberty, Commerce, Labour and Art and is seen in these views looking from Vicar Lane to Briggate. Before being incorporated into the city's prestigious Victoria Quarter the Arcade underwent considerable restoration and reconstruction work in 1989/1990 funded by Prudential Portfolio Managers.

BRIGGATE AND THE EMPIRE PALACE THEATRE

Briggate is now pedestrianised, security cameras have been installed, and the thoroughfare is no longer part of the public transport system. Missing from the east side of the street is the Empire Palace Theatre. Designed by renowned theatre architect, Frank Matcham, the building opened on August 29, 1898 and seventeen acts were featured. From 1931, cinematograph equipment was installed but stage shows also continued. This lasted until the final show – Emile Littler's 'Babes in the Wood' starring Nat Jackley – on February 25, 1961. The building was demolished in the following year and the site redeveloped.

BRIGGATE LOOKING SOUTH

An idea of the traffic congestion caused by trams, delivery vehicles and parked cars can be gleaned in the top view along Briggate facing south to the junctions with Duncan Street and Boar Lane. An impression of how buildings have been disfigured by commercial premises and then demolished is also gathered by comparing both pictures. In the old picture the double-gabled premises on the right dated from 1613 and were built by Richard Sykes, Alderman of Leeds in 1629. Timpsons' Shoes took over the premises in 1919, demolished them in 1955 and built a new shop. Thus, commercial redevelopment on this section of Briggate has been quite dramatic and far reaching with many of the larger, well-known high street names swamping the area.

BRIGGATE, PICTURE HOUSE

The Picture House (Rialto from 4 February 1927) had a relatively short life-span, even for a cinema. Mrs Curer Briggs, wife of a former Lord Mayor of Leeds, opened the building on Tuesday afternoon, April 4, 1911. The proprietor was John Smith Ltd, the lessee, Provincial Cinematograph Theatres Ltd. Closure occurred following the showing of 'Woman Teaser', starring George Raft and Joan Blondell, on March 11, 1939. Once cleared, the cinema site was occupied by Marks & Spencer.

BRIGGATE, WOOLWORTH'S

New York-born, Frank W. Woolworth (1852-1919) opened his first UK store in Liverpool on November 6, 1909. Premises were added in Leeds' Exchange Buildings during 1910. By the beginning of the First World War, Woolworth & Co. had around 40 stores in Great Britain and Ireland. To make way for the second Woolworth's in Leeds the Albion Hotel was demolished on the east side of Briggate. Opening on December 1, 1928, the building suffered a major fire during 1969. Closure came in 1987 and by early 2009 over 800 Woolworth's stores had closed. The Woolworth's Briggate site was subsequently occupied by House of Fraser.

CALL LANE, CORN EXCHANGE

An earlier Corn Exchange existed at the top of Briggate between 1827 and the mid-19th century. A new building, oval in plan, was designed by Cuthbert Brodrick and built by Samuel Addy and Butler & Co. (who constructed the roof). Completed in 1862, the structure's total cost was around £25,000. Corn farmers and corn factors conducted their business in the large first floor area. The two-storey building underwent a major refurbishment in 1985 which was undertaken by Specialist Shops PLC and then reopened to the public around 1990 as a retail centre. This includes quality shops located around the balcony area. The Corn Exchange is Listed Grade I.

CALVERLEY STREET, FACING NORTH

Calverley Street was extended northwards in 1914 to join Fenton Street. The Leeds General Infirmary Brotherton wing, financed by Charles Frederick Ratcliffe Brotherton (1882-1949) at a cost of £50,000, was built in Portland Stone and opened on November 14, 1940. The Civic Hall in the centre was also erected in Portland Stone to the designs of E.V. Harris. The building was opened in 1933 by King George V and Queen Mary. Since the top picture was taken, the area presently forms the Millennium Square which was one of Leeds' main projects to mark the year 2000. Since then, the Square has become a focal point for events in the city centre. The buildings on the right – Portland Chambers, Stansfield Chambers and the Electric Press building were converted to house the Carriageworks Theatre (opened November 15, 2005) as well as bars and restaurants.

CENTRAL ROAD/NEW MARKET STREET

Vallance's electrical business was begun by Alec Vallance in a shop in Scunthorpe during 1934. From there, the business grew to include over 40 shops and out of town stores, turning over £50m per year. The firm was always based predominantly in Yorkshire but did have outlets in the Midlands and Lancashire. The Central Road/New Market Street store is pictured here on November 21, 1972. Alec Vallance's son, Martin sold the business in 1987 to Thorn EMI.

CITY SQUARE, WELLINGTON STREET/PARK ROW JUNCTION

The top picture was taken by Wormald c. 1890 and shows Wellington Street on the left with the West Riding Hotel at no. 38; the five-storey Quebec Buildings, occupied by woollen manufacturers Newsome, West & Co. Ltd; the Coloured Cloth Hall, in the centre with a dome; the old Post Office; and Park Row. None of the buildings survive today, the area being completely remodelled following the building of the new Post Office and the creation of City Square. A direct route from Park Row to Wellington Street has also been broken by these developments.

BLACK PRINCE STATUE, LEEDS.

CITY SQUARE – THE BLACK PRINCE

All around the Black Prince extensive alterations have occurred but his proud effigy still dominates City Square which remains an impressive spectacle, despite some rearrangements, for both Leeds residents and visitors. Industrialist Colonel Thomas Walter Harding commissioned the Black Prince sculpture. He proposed and financed a number of sculptures when the City Square was remodelled to create an open space in commemoration of Leeds' elevation from town to city in 1893. The Black Prince project was entrusted to sculptor Thomas Brock (1847–1922). The bronze was unveiled in front of thousands of spectators at noon, September 16, 1903.

CITY SQUARE CLASSIC CINEMA

A cinema named the News Theatre, incorporated within the Queen's Hotel, opened on Monday 22, August 1938. With seating for a mere 290, the premises specialised in up to the minute news, showing Pathe News and cartoons. Afterwards, the premises underwent a number of name changes: Classic; Tatler Film Club; and once more as the Classic. The above photograph was taken shortly before closure in January 1981, but the building reopened several months later for a two-week film festival. Afterwards the building housed a nightclub, Bondi Beach Bar, for a short period.

CITY SQUARE LOOKING TO PARK ROW

On the left in the top picture is no. 1 City Square occupied by the Standard Life Assurance building, completed in 1901. New property, opening for the Norwich Union on the site in March 1967, courted controversy being subsequently voted one of Britain's ugliest buildings before demolition in 1995. Norwich Union erected a new building on the site in 1996 to the designs of Abbey Hanson Rowe. On the right is the Priestley Hall, demolished in 1968 for the construction of the NatWest building, Priestley House. Currently occupying the site after the demolition of the NatWest property is No. 1 Park Row, officially opened in April 2000 and designed by Fletcher Joseph. The Mill Hill Unitarian Chapel, to the right, was opened in December 1948 and is the only survivor from the earlier view.

CITY SQUARE GENERAL POST OFFICE BUILDING

Leeds City Square General Post Office was designed by Sir Henry Tanner (1835-1924) and built in 1896 on the site of an old cloth hall. He was noted for designing a series of head post offices in Britain in a style often referred to as 'Northern Renaissance'. The Leeds building was originally the city's largest Post Office and also served as a telephone exchange. Since the top picture was taken the building no longer fulfils its original function. The interior was renovated at a cost of approx. £8 million in 2006 and presently houses Residence 6, luxury holiday apartments, with restaurants and bars on the ground floor.

CITY SQUARE, QUEEN'S HOTEL

Railway hotels were a prominent feature of Victorian travel. Railway companies proudly erected them at termini stations or crucial connecting points. The Midland Railway Company opened the Queen's Hotel in Leeds adjacent to their railway station on January 10, 1863. It was designed by Perkin & Blackhouse and new wings were added in 1867 and 1898. In 1923 the Midland Railway was absorbed into the London Midland & Scottish Railway Company and by November 1937 a new Queen's Hotel had opened. The Art Deco style of the building was considered to symbolise the transition of Leeds from a parochial Victorian city to a national centre.

COMMERCIAL STREET

Noted Leeds architect, George Corson, designed the building featured here in his favoured Gothic style for Harvey, Reynolds & Co. in 1868. The site had a long history of being associated with chemists. When Thomas Harvey died in December 1884, Reynolds took on Frederick Branson as partner. An advert around this time stated the company were manufacturers and exporters of chemical apparatus. The company also dealt with pure chemicals and reagents, laboratory fittings and furniture, optical lanterns and slides, and photographic apparatus. Later the company, which had other premises in Briggate, underwent a number of personnel changes, surviving until the 1970s. It is unfortunate that the lower part of the building has been lost.

COMMERCIAL STREET

Extending between Bond Street and Briggate, Commercial Street is shown facing east. The thoroughfare was created in 1806, primarily as a means of providing a good route from Kirkgate to the town's west side. Burt and Grady in *The Illustrated History of Leeds* (1994) mention that the elegant Commercial Street, 'one of the most commodious avenues into Briggate' was initially known as Bond Street.

Throughout much of the 19th century the area was part of the boom in well designed, ornate commercial/business properties. But, even by the late 19th century there were traffic congestion problems 'on the busiest days and at the busiest times' caused by a variety of vehicles; pedestrianisation did not occur until 1970. Although largely a haunt of the affluent middle classes during the 19th century, Commercial Street is presently frequented by a wider variety of people.

COOKRIDGE STREET/WOODHOUSE LANE JUNCTION

The top picture was taken on January 18, 1967 at the time when traffic lights were being erected at the Cookridge Street/Woodhouse Lane junction. The three-storey premises are occupied, from l to r, by Davies Ltd, leather goods and saddlery; Dinsdale, drawing materials and bookshop; Alfred Weaver, menswear. Almost out of view on the left are premises once occupied by A. & H. Supplies (Hardware) Ltd. To the right, on Woodhouse Lane, is a barbers shop and a white-wood furniture store. All these buildings have been swept away and for a period the vacant area was used as a car park. It is now planned to open a hotel on the site, work being seen in progress in the picture below.

COOKRIDGE STREET

The Leeds Institute was completed in 1862 to the designs of Cuthbert Brodrick. The purpose of the building was to provide education facilities for the city's industrial workers and a venue for lectures and large scale events. Between 1949 and 2005 it housed the Civic Theatre, allowing amateur theatrical groups to stage public performances. When the purpose-built Carriageworks Theatre opened nearby in November 2005, these groups and others transferred to this building. Following a major refurbishment, funded by Leeds council and the Heritage Lottery Fund, the former Leeds Institute is presently occupied by Leeds Museum, formerly accommodated, until 1999, in municipal buildings, along with the Central Library, in Calverley Street.

COOKRIDGE STREET

Cuthbert Brodrick designed this block of commercial premises – shops and offices – at 49-51 Cookridge Street in 1864. They are commonly known as Brodrick's Buildings and belong to a rare group of smaller commercial premises he designed in his idiosyncratic Gothic style. Four other drawings executed in the same year were provided for Hull St John (now demolished); Leeds Headingley Hill Congregational Church; London Natural History Museum (an unsuccessful competition entry). Looking rather run down in the top picture, dating from November 22, 1985, the buildings were subsequently transformed in the intervening years to form a vibrant bar.

COOKRIDGE STREET, AUSTICK'S

Bertie Austick was a partner in Massey's Bookshop in Lower Headrow until the company went into liquidation in 1928. Wife Hilda and himself started their own book business and were eventually joined by their two sons, Paul and David. Bertie died in 1938 but the three family members continued. Steady expansion followed until there were nine shops in Leeds and Harrogate. There were also stores in Scarborough and Huddersfield Technical College. The company closed in 1998, the ensuing years not being kind to independent book retailers. Thus, former city bookshop premises, like Austick's in Cookridge Street, are presently occupied by industries managing to juggle profits more successfully with high commercial rents and leases.

CROWN STREET

A building once known as the Third White Cloth Hall is seen above and below at 27 and 27A Crown Street. Dating from around 1776 the premises were used by weavers to market their un-dyed and unfinished cloth. Accommodating approx. 1,213 stalls these were laid out inside the building which included a large central courtyard. Part of the Third White Cloth Hall was taken in railway developments during 1868 and a fourth hall was erected in King Street. Yet, by this time the industry was in decline because of changes in the marketing of cloth. Thereafter, a variety of uses were found for several of the cloth halls and the one seen here has been divided into units.

DUNCAN STREET

Duncan Street looking west to the Holy Trinity Church in Boar Lane. The thoroughfare was originally titled Fleet Street then Duncan Street after Admiral Viscount Duncan's victory at Camperdown during October 1797.

Between c.1824 and 1893 an area on Duncan Street's northern side was occupied by the Central Market. Fire damage resulted in the area being cleared and the street line set back. Architects involved in designing the new buildings included Percy Robinson. As can be gathered from the top picture, Duncan Street once formed an integral part of the tram system and it continues to play an equally important part today in the public transport network. Judging from the number of To Let signs seen in the modern picture it might suggest Duncan Street has become something of a backwater following the establishment of shopping malls in various areas around the city.

EAST PARADE, LEEDS. 560/464.

EAST PARADE

Fowler's Plan of Leeds, 1821 only shows buildings present on the west side of East Parade – developed 1779-1789. Plots may be seen laid out on the east side and these were subsequently occupied as the thoroughfare became an important part of the city now known as the Financial Quarter. A proportion of the west side is presently swallowed up in the No. 1 East Parade development being an example of a style known as 'the Leeds Look', instantly recognised by the use of dark red brick and steeply pitched grey roofs.

EAST PARADE CHAPEL

Here we see an area changing from religious to commercial use. The East Parade Congregational Chapel, designed in a Doric style by William Hurst and W.L. Moffatt, dated from 1841. Seating was for 1,600. The top picture was taken by Wormald with Greek Street on the left and Russell Street to the right. Closure of the Chapel occurred on July 23, 1899 and following demolition soon afterwards the site accommodated a new building belonging to the North British & Mercantile Insurance Co. These premises featured ornate stone window surrounds and an elaborate stone front including two arched porches. In turn the site was redeveloped in 1966 and once again during the 1990s, presently accommodating Minerva House.

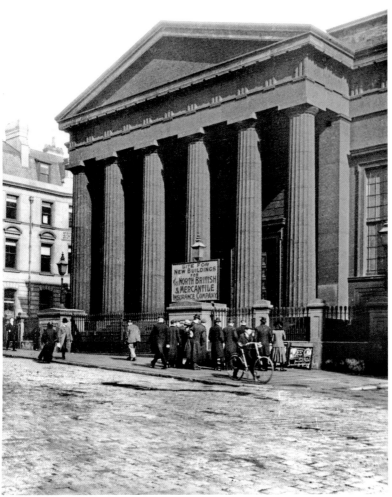

EAST PARADE GREEK STREET CORNER

Shown here is the East Parade/Greek Street corner; the dominating premises in the top picture are occupied on the ground floor by the Alliance Assurance Company; the first floor by Crawford's Solicitors; and the second by the Vulcan Boiler & General insurance offices. Presently, the redeveloped site is occupied by Yorkshire House with the East Parade/Greek Street corner ground floor tenanted by All Bar One. This is one corner of Leeds where public opinion will be divided on whether the area looks better or worse for the changes which have occurred over the years. Situated in the heart of the city's business district, Yorkshire House has recently undergone a major refurbishment and modernisation programme. Publicity blurb states this is 'to reflect the finest in modern business space design, functionality and environment'.

GREAT GEORGE STREET

The foundation stone for St George's Church was laid by the Bishop of Ripon on December 16, 1836 and the building was completed around two years later. Designed by John Clark, the church features a west tower with spire. During 1930, the church began a new chapter in its life when vicar Don Robins established a sanctuary for the homeless in the crypt. This work continues today, with the Church providing support for the homeless and asylum seekers. Along with running hostels, as well as charity shops, the church organises events and programmes for people struggling to cope with addictions. In the distance on the right is the Leeds School of Medicine, designed by W.H. Thorpe and opened in 1894.

GREAT GEORGE STREET

Leeds' first General Infirmary was built on Infirmary Street 1768-1781 replacing temporary accommodation in William Hey's House in Kirkgate. A new building occupying a site in Great George Street was designed by Sir George Gilbert Scott. The foundation stone was laid on March 29, 1864 and the building opened on May 22, 1869. The inspiration for Scott's design is alleged to have been derived from him visiting French hospitals. An East wing, on the right, was added in 1891/2 to the designs of George Corson. Inside, medical practices have altered dramatically over the years, even since the top picture was taken on October 2, 1967, but externally the building has remained virtually unaltered for over 100 years. Motor car development quite noticeably has moved on apace.

HEADROW LOOKING TO THE TOWN HALL

The newly widened Headrow – a section of the northern side is seen here looking north-west – was completed between 1928 and 1932. The first building to open along the new thoroughfare was the Leeds Permanent Building Society's headquarters on May 15, 1930. The banking hall was said to be a 'magnificently' appointed room. A main feature of the whole development was the white Portland Stone chosen in an attempt to resist the blackening by soot which affected a good many of the city's buildings. Initially, after the introduction of pedestrianisation and the planting of trees and shrubs to the Headrow it was nicknamed 'The Hedgerow'. The Leeds Permanent Building Society's headquarters moved to a new building in Lovell Park Road around 1990.

HEADROW WIDENING LOOKING EAST

The top picture illustrates the Upper Headrow, looking east, before the widening scheme took place. Premises demolished include those belonging to J.R. Teale & Son, cabinetmakers and upholsterers; the General Electric Co; and Beacock, chemist. The thoroughfare was widened between 1928 and 1932 in a plan designed by architect Reginald Blomfield as a means of improving traffic flow through the city centre. Large commercial premises, seen on the left in the bottom picture, on the set back street line, were formerly occupied by John Lewis's Department Store (opening on 17 September 1932), then Allders. It presently houses branches of T.K. Maxx, Argos and Sainsbury's, among others.

HEADROW WIDENING LOOKING WEST

In the top picture all the properties to the right were demolished for the Headrow widening scheme. These included business premises occupied by Schofield, confectioner; Skelton, hosier and shirt maker; and Wm Brownfoot, sunblinds. Plans for the widened thoroughfare were put to Leeds Council's improvement committee in May 1924, but work did not start until approx. two years later because of land ownership disputes. The new road, including pavements, was 80 feet wide and was completed at a cost of £500,000. In 1974 plans were introduced to pedestrianise the Headrow whereby access was only allowed for buses, taxis and delivery vehicles. Despite much opposition from traders the plan was carried out.

HEADROW, THE PARAMOUNT

The Paramount Cinema, designed by London architect, Frank T. Verity, for proprietors Paramount Theatre Ltd, opened at 7pm on Monday February 22, 1932. Becoming the Odeon on April 15, 1940, the venue also staged live shows with the Beatles playing there in June 1963, November 1963 and October 1964. Two screens were run from May 15, 1969 and Odeon 3 opened on Sunday July 23, 1978. But, this could not avert closure, which occurred on October 28, 2001. Designated Grade II, the building has since been converted to housing on the upper floor and a Primark clothing store at ground level.

HEADROW SCHOFIELDS

Snowden Schofield arrived in Leeds from his native Bradford in 1901 and established a business in the Victoria Arcade, along the Headrow. Over the ensuing years, he added more Arcade shops to his business and developed other adjacent areas on the Headrow. In 1947, the whole of the Victoria Arcade was purchased and Snowden died two years later. In 1961, the entire Schofield's site, including land in Lands Lane, The Headrow and King Charles Street, was redeveloped, by Snowden's sons, into a new store. Another scheme begun in 1987 saw Schofield's Shopping Centre emerge around three years later. Schofield's on The Headrow closed on July 27, 1996, the complex is presently known as The Core.

HEADROW TOWN HALL

Cuthbert Brodrick won a competition in 1852 held to find a design for the new Leeds Town Hall. The tender of Samuel Atack was accepted for the erection of the building. When completed the Town Hall had a number of uses: for Leeds council; judicial functions; as a police station; to provide a hall for musical concerts and civic functions. Today, the Town Hall only houses a small number of council offices but continues to provide a venue for many different types of concerts. It is no longer a police station and does not provide courts. Black soot and grime was removed from the building during the 1970s and it still stands as a magnificent statement of civic pride.

HEADROW/VICAR LANE CORNER

Dating from April 25, 1936, the top picture was taken prior to the construction of Lloyds Bank designed by Sir Reginald Blomfield at The Headrow/Vicar Lane corner. Other former traders include, on Vicar Lane: H. Wigfall & Son and Hartley's Music Stores. Also visible is the Nag's Head Hotel. Seen on The Headrow are Philips Stores; H. Brown & Sons; Waldenberg Bros; and The Pram shop. The Lloyds Bank building has achieved Listed status while the Nag's Head (on the extreme left in the top picture) closed in August 2003. Landlord John Mitchell served the last pint when it was owned by Leeds-based company Musgrave & Sagar.

INFIRMARY STREET

Infirmary Street takes its name from being the first thoroughfare to be occupied by Leeds General Infirmary. The street is depicted here looking north-west where the east side has undergone considerable redevelopment. The triangular building on the right, Gordon Chambers, was formerly tenanted by a number of firms including the Yorkshire Insurance Company. On the left, a stretch of buildings once attached to the Post Office were cleared c. 1980 and subsequently accommodated new premises, Cloth Hall Court, erected 1980-1983. The building with the tower is the old Yorkshire Penny Bank Building, designed by George Bertram Bulmer and built in 1894 on the site of the old infirmary.

KING STREET

The east side of King Street once housed the Fourth White Cloth Hall, erected in 1865 but demolished in 1895. The Hotel Metropole was erected on the site and the Cloth Hall's cupola was incorporated into the new building. Designed broadly in French Loire taste by Chorley, Cannon & Chorley, the Metropole opened on June 28, 1899 and was built in pink/red brick and terracotta, manufactured by J.C. Edwards of Ruabon. The pillared entrance features intricate details moulded in clay. The top picture dates from October 1973 and during March of the following year, the Metropole was Listed Grade II. After undergoing an approx. £6m refurbishment in 2005, under the Principal Hayley Group, the premises adopted the simpler, and perhaps trendier title of 'The Met.'

KIRKGATE

The main change to occur here in a view looking south-east to Leeds Minster is the building of a new Market Hall; part of the old premises are seen on the left in the above picture c. 1900. Towards the mid-1800s moves were made towards the erection of a Market Hall through the establishment of a Market Committee which purchased additional lands and gained approval for the demolition of slums in the immediate vicinity. In mid-1857 the Hall, erected from iron and glass, was completed, being designed by C. Tilney with input from Sir Joseph Paxton of Crystal Palace fame. Further expansion occurred in the 1870s as buildings for traders outside the market hall were provided. The old building on the left was removed with the construction of a new Market Hall c. 1904.

KIRKGATE

One of Leeds' oldest streets, Kirkgate, is depicted facing north-west from New Market Street/Vicar Lane, to the junction with Central Road (on the left) and Briggate/Commercial Street beyond. The first surviving plan of Leeds (1560) actually shows this stretch of Kirkgate existing during that period. Once noted business premises on the south side in the top picture include those belonging to Tiffany; Best & Booth; and Vassalli & Co. Ltd. As in a number of other streets in and around the city, many of the ground floor premises have no connection with the upper floors. Perhaps the main and beneficial change to occur – for shoppers at least – in the intervening years is the pedestrianisation scheme.

KIRKGATE

In the top picture looking towards Briggate, Kirkgate is bustling with activity and the buildings present an exciting, commercial appearance to the streetscape. The north side features Lipton's and the Theatre de Luxe (with Sloans Billiards on an upper floor). The Theatre de Luxe seated 383 patrons and existed between 1910-1934. Lipton's tea brand and chain of stores was founded by Thomas Lipton (1848-1931), who began with a small provision shop in Glasgow during 1871. Lipton grocery stores were then established in Scotland and throughout Britain eventually being merged with a number of other concerns in 1929. The Lipton Tea business was later acquired by Unilever.

KIRKGATE

The two views are separated by 41 years, the top one taken February 25, 1974, the bottom, March 2015, yet the shop fronts and the rest of the buildings show little maintenance has occurred. Hopefully, this will change over the ensuing years, as the Lower Kirkgate area became the subject of a recent Leeds Council Planning Statement. This was seen as an appropriate way to agree 'basic objectives and parameters for the sensitive regeneration and restoration of this area.'

The statement also informs that Kirkgate, being the historic core of Leeds, has been the site of continuous development since at least the Anglo-Saxon period.

KIRKGATE

Above, the business premises of E. Jackson, scale-maker are identified at the Cross York Street corner, demolished c. 1908. On the opposite side, at the Wharf Street junction, is no. 76 Kirkgate formerly the business premises of Matt Botterill, clothier. A section of the North Eastern Railway Co's bridge is seen top left in both pictures. In the distance, Leeds Parish Church, dedicated to St Peter, was designed by Robert Chantrell and built in 1838-41 under the auspices of the Vicar of Leeds Dr W.F. Hook. It replaced an earlier church with roots back to at least 1086 that was altered, enlarged and rebuilt over the medieval period as Leeds grew into a busy market town. The 'new' Parish Church became a Minster in 2012 and has achieved Grade II Listed status.

LANDS LANE

The Lands Lane name is derived from fields or lands belonging to the Lord of the Manor of Leeds. The top view illustrates the street looking towards Commercial Street c. 1898. Around this time, and into the 20th century, Lands Lane experienced considerable upheaval with widening and rebuilding schemes. Business premises top left include those belonging to Allpass & Co., Home Furnishers; and Thomas Mallorie & Co., wine and spirits merchants. Noticeable on the right is scaffolding for the construction of Victoria Arcade. When Lands Lane and Commercial Street were paved from November 1970 this, it was believed, according to Burt and Grady, created 'the largest pedestrianised shopping street in Europe'.

LANDS LANE

On the right above, is the Victoria Arcade, built in 1898 to commemorate Queen Victoria's Jubilee. Designed by Thomas Ambler, it was L-shaped, extended through from Lands Lane to the Headrow and was erected for commercial property owner F. W. Dawson. There were 26 large shop units, including show rooms on the ground floor and work rooms above. The arcade was demolished in 1959 but as mentioned by Christopher Webster (ed) in *Building a Great Victorian City* (2011) if the Victoria Arcade had survived 'it would have undoubtedly become a site for 'bijou' shopping to rival the County Arcade'.

LANDS LANE

Running between the Headrow and Commercial Street, Lands Lane once had quite a number of well-known premises on its western side. Amongst these were the Theatre Royal and Schofield's. A theatre on the site can be traced back to 1848 but after a number of developments, the Theatre Royal opened in 1876. Noted Theatre manager, Francis Laidler became lessee in 1909 and thereafter, the Theatre Royal earned a reputation for staging some of the most successful pantomimes in the north of England. Laidler died in 1955 and his wife struggled on for a further two years, the last performance occurring on March 30, 1957. After being sold to Schofield's the building was demolished. The site is now part of the Headrow Shopping Centre; Lands Lane was pedestrianised in November 1970.

MERRION CENTRE

In the Leeds 1951 Development Plan, the area later occupied by the Merrion Centre was originally intended to provide a multi-storey car park and bus station. On May 26, 1964, Arnold Ziff, chairman of Town Centre Securities Ltd, opened his new £6,000,000 Merrion Centre in front of over 1,000 invited guests. In early 1960s Leeds, having a 'city-within-a-city', was groundbreaking. It was the largest indoor shopping centre in the UK and a pioneering development combining shops with leisure activities in a vehicle-free environment. The Merrion Centre's pedestrian precincts and multi-storey car park were very much firsts for England.

MERRION CENTRE

Arnold Ziff said the Merrion Centre, designed by Gillinson, Barnett & Partners, was situated in the city centre adjoining the traditional shopping centre and the two largest stores (Lewis's Limited and Schofield's Ltd). A leaflet published by The Merrion Centre, 1964 gives the following details: 'There are 68,000 cubic yards of excavated material, of which 20,000 cubic yards are rock, and this would fill the 13-storey Wade House office building approximately 1½ times. The total weight of the buildings, excluding the car park, is 42,000 tons, which is equivalent to twice the weight of the Cunard steamship *Carinthia*, or slightly more than the weight of the *Mauretania*.'

MILL HILL, BLACK LION

Like a number of other pubs in the city, the curved, red-brick three-storey Black Lion, has undergone a number of name changes. Before holding its present title, Head of Steam, it was also known as Spencer's and was formerly tied to the Tetley estate. It was refurbished by Joshua Tetley's in 1993 at a cost of £230,000. The premises became part of the Head of Steam branded pubs (owned by Cameron's) in 2014 and after some years of neglect much has been done – via a six-figure refurbishment – to shake off its slightly unsavoury image from the past.

NEW BRIGGATE

Looking north along New Briggate, the upper photograph, taken c. 1928, features business premises occupied by Allan Schofield, tobacconist; and Edward Skelton, hosier. All the buildings, extending to the entrance to St John the Evangelist's Church, being demolished for the erection of Lewis's. The Leeds site cost Lewis's £160,000 and involved the demolition of a number of old yards. The company had other stores in Liverpool, Manchester, Birmingham and Glasgow. Lewis's Leeds island site covered an area of 6,067 sq. yards and constructional engineers Edward Wood & Co. Ltd were amongst those responsible for the building work.

NEW BRIGGATE

Looking south, from near Mark Lane along Briggate to the Headrow junction business premises identified in the top picture, taken c. 1928, include those belonging to Greenhills and Halford Cycle Co. Ltd. All the properties were demolished for Lewis's store. David Lewis founded his own business in Liverpool in 1856 with the aim of supplying good quality clothing to the working man and his family. Branching out into home furnishings, turned into a desire to establish department stores. Nephew Louis Cohen, took control after his uncle's death and with the help of Frederick James Marquis, further expansion in the company took place. The Leeds store cost around three-quarters of a million pounds.

NEW BRIGGATE/MERRION STREET CORNER

Looking at G.E. Taylor's rather unique shop, shown in the left-hand picture, perhaps clearly illustrates this kind of niche business – offering services for setting, sharpening and repairing saws – can no longer survive on this scale in the city. Taken c. 1929, the picture was perhaps a means of recording the corner before a substantial development took place shortly afterwards in the form of a large four-storey building. Whilst lamenting the loss of G.E. Taylor's specialist business from the city's street, the modern picture reveals that certain kinds of niche markets can still thrive even today on this corner. The IT Bar and Food Joint provides free Wi-Fi, live music, and DJs on deck duty spinning the best Funk, Rock, Disco, Alternative, Boogie, and Balearic music. Also on offer are gastronomic delights, many different types of drinks and all, as the website states 'until the wee small hours'.

NEW BRIGGATE, THE GRAND THEATRE

Designed by George Corson with assistance from James Robertson Watson, the Grand Theatre opened on November 18, 1878 at a cost of £62,000. Leeds Council bought the theatre in 1973 and major refurbishment of the building costing around £31.5 million began in 2005 and was completed in the following year. The Grand is presently the home of English National Opera North and the Northern Ballet Theatre.

NEW BRIGGATE

The Grand Arcade was converted into a picture house, the Tower Cinema, which opened on April 12, 1920. The conversion plans were executed by architect J.P. Crawford and seating was for 1,188. Run by the New Briggate Picture House Ltd., the cinema was later taken over by the local chain Tower Picture House (Leeds) Ltd. A Western Electric sound system was installed during 1930. Closure came in 1985 and the premises were initially converted to a nightclub and, in time, the BED Club/ Gatecrasher venue. Presently, they house The Brotherhood or to give it its full title, The Brotherhood of Pastimes and Pursuits. It is the latest in a long line of interesting new venues to pop up in Leeds' burgeoning Northern Quarter.

NEW MARKET STREET

New Market Street, created by the Improvement Commissioners in 1833, is located between Kirkgate and Duncan Street. Taken during the 1950s, the top picture shows the days of the tramway era. Car no 228, off-centre to the right, is working on the Beeston service (no. 5); no. 513, extreme right to Compton Road (no. 10). Car no. 513 was one of the Feltham's vehicles, so named because they were built by the Union Construction Company in Feltham. Whilst many of the commercial premises have changed tenants and uses the area still features strongly in the city's transport system. Modern buses it may be argued provide a better standard of facilities and comfort than the electric trams.

PARK ROW

Looking north in the top picture, St Anne's Cathedral, in the distance on Guildford Street (presently The Headrow), was demolished in 1904 and rebuilt on Cookridge Street. Park Row was once part of the Park Estate made up of fields and owned by the Wilson family. When the family granted a building lease in 1767 for residential development, Park Row was built shortly afterwards. The street was wide, with terraces of large houses occupied by the leading families of Leeds. When other streets were developed at the dawn of the 19th century, the area was transformed into a business district. Families along Park Row gradually moved out to escape the industrialisation of the city with its inherent smog, soot, increased traffic and infectious diseases; their properties converted to commercial premises.

PARK ROW

The Builder Magazine of December 19, 1896 described Park Row as the 'Pall Mall of Leeds' because of the cluster of banks and insurance companies along the thoroughfare. All of this had occurred through much of the 19th century. The financial institutions occupied impressive buildings designed by very competent architects including George Corson and Alfred Waterhouse. Some of them still survive, whilst others have been lost and their sites redeveloped for even more commercial institutions to take root. But, in recent years several financial buildings after becoming redundant have been redeveloped as bars and restaurants. Park Row has long been part of the city's transport system, electric trams travelled along the street, as may be seen in the top picture, and then they were superseded by motor buses – now provided with bus lanes.

QUEBEC STREET

Named after General Wolfe – captor of Quebec in Canada in 1759 – Quebec Street opened 13 years later. The top picture dates from October 1973 and, over the intervening 42 years, extensive alterations have taken place on both sides of the street. On the left a building erected 1980-1983 is part of the Cloth Hall Court complex, accommodating various businesses besides the Leeds Metropolitan University's Law School. Opposite, the 47,000 sq. ft premises were built for Walker Morris, the Leeds-based solicitors in 1989. In the distance the old Leeds and County Liberal Club, built in 1891 to the designs of Chorley and Connon, was partially converted to offices in 1921 then fully from 1947, but is now Quebecs Hotel.

REGENT STREET/NEW YORK ROAD FLYOVER

After suffering severe traffic congestion, because Leeds was on the main route joining cities west and east, it was decided in the mid-1950s to build an inner relief road to ease traffic passing through the city. Starting in the early 1960s, the road was built in stages. The top picture shows the New York Road flyover – part of the Inner Relief Road – under construction near Regent Street and Quarry Hill Flats in a photograph dated June 1969. According to the *Civil Engineering and Public Works Review* (1969) the bridge, lying on massive concrete pillars, was difficult to build: 'piling was necessary at both abutments and piers of the Regent Street Flyover where boreholes were taken down to 100ft without meeting any hard strata'.

THIRSK ROW

The short stretch of Thirsk Row was the centre of a national event on June 20, 1911 but thereafter slipped back into relative obscurity. The first trolleybuses to run in Britain started on that day in both Leeds and Bradford. Originally the inaugural Leeds trip was to begin from City Square. But, at the last moment, it was decided that, as a large crowd might considerably impede traffic at this point, it would be better the assembly of the Corporation and their guests should take place in some less frequented thoroughfare. Thus, two vehicles nos 501 and 503 were drawn up in Thirsk Row. The Lord Mayor William Middlebrook M.P. was in one car and Alderman Kitson in the other. The Leeds trolleybuses were not a success and were withdrawn by 1929; the last one ran in Bradford in 1972.

VICAR LANE

When Leeds became a city in 1893, councillors wanted public areas to reflect this new importance and, while City Square was the first development to be instigated, the improvement of the market was seen as equally pressing. A competition was staged in 1899 for designs of a new covered market. Leeming Brothers of London, designers of buildings in Halifax and admired by the Market Committee, won the contest with a Market Hall projected to cost £73,000. Work began in 1901 and was finished in 1904. The Market has continued to develop over the years and was partly rebuilt following the fire of 1975 where two thirds of the market buildings were destroyed. With approx. 800 stalls and around 100,000 people visiting on Saturdays, Leeds Market continues to be one of the largest in Europe.

VICAR LANE, EASTMANS/PRAGUE

Eastmans Leeds was part of a large chain and there were approx. 1,700 outlets by 1914. T.C. Eastman was a New Yorker and shipped cattle to a John Bell of Glasgow. John Bell had opened shops in the name of The American Fresh Meat Co with over 300 by 1889. A year later Bell and Eastman established Eastmans. 500 stores were closed due to lack of meat and staff during WWI. Then, 1,200 stores were sold to Vestey in 1922 to add to their empire. Quite remarkably, the design of the shop frontage design remains much the same now as did in Eastmans' time. It is also encouraging to see independent retailers such as Prague (footwear) thriving in such a prestigious location as the Grade I Listed Market frontage.

VICAR LANE MARKET INTERIOR

Sometimes it is difficult to date old pictures unless there are significant clues. There is one major clue for dating the left-hand picture. It was taken between 1904, when the New Market Hall opened, and July 1912, when the clock tower was removed. Designed by John and Joseph Leeming of London, the clock was built by Potts & Son of Leeds at a cost of £150. It was moved by Leeds Parks Department to provide ease of access to and from a new central market entrance being opened on Vicar Lane. Finding a new home in Roundhay Park, at the junction of Roundhay Road and Princess Avenue, the Oakwood Clock, as it became known, underwent restoration in 1977.

VICAR LANE, VICTORIA QUARTER

The major change to occur here is the stained glass roof, designed by Brian Clarke, thrown over the full length of Queen Victoria Street, to form, along with the County and Cross Arcades, the Victoria Quarter. This was undertaken by the Prudential towards the end of the 1980s when the area had fallen into commercial decay. The glass roof is featured in the Guinness Book of Records as the largest stained glass window in Britain. Winning an accolade in the Leeds Awards for Architecture in 1991, the Victoria Quarter presently contains a clever blend of old and new.

VICAR LANE RITZ/ABC CINEMA

Associated Cinemas Ltd opened the Ritz on Monday, November 19, 1934, with seating available for 1,100 in the stalls and 850 in the circle. 'Those Were the Days' was the first film shown. A name-change to ABC occurred from May 23, 1959. The premises were twinned on April 5, 1970 until Sunday March 17, 1974, when ABC 2 was divided into two screens. Becoming the Cannon in March 1987, the MGM in 1991, then back to ABC in 1993, closure came in February 2000. Screen 1 showed 'American Beauty', screen 2 'Double Jeopardy' and the Bollywood film 'Shaheed Uddham Singh' in screen 3. The building was razed to the ground in February 2006.

VICAR LANE BUS STATION

Laid out on the site of the old workhouse and north bar, the Vicar Lane or West Yorkshire Bus Station opened 1936/37. Dominating the views are the booking and enquiry offices of motor coach proprietors the West Yorkshire Road Car Company Ltd, established in 1927 but its origins trace back to 1906. By 1948 the company was state owned and c. 1968 was transferred to the National Bus Company. Following a management buy-out, West Yorkshire was split into smaller companies during around 1988, and sold to Blazefield holdings in 1991. Closure of the Vicar Lane Red Bus Station – as it was known to some – occurred on March 31, 1990 and all services were transferred to the Central Bus Station. The vacant Vicar Lane bus station area is presently used as a car park.

VICAR LANE/HEADROW CORNER

Lloyds Bank was established in Birmingham by Samuel Lloyd during 1765 as Taylor & Lloyds Banking Co. Ltd. Lloyds began trading in Leeds during 1900 and the original premises at the Vicar Lane/Headrow corner dated from 1906-1908. They are seen here c.1928. A new bank building – set back to a new street line around 1930 – was designed in accordance with a uniform style adopted for the Headrow by Sir Reginald Blomfield. The premises are currently Listed.

VICAR LANE

Vicar Lane is seen looking south to Sidney Street (on the left) from the junction with the Headrow. The top picture was taken shortly after the east side was set back, widening the street from 27 feet to 75 feet. This occurred during the last decade of the 19th century to deal with the increase in the flow of traffic particularly around the market area. New buildings constructed on Vicar Lane included Coronation Buildings in 1904 and the County Hotel. Many people would agree the widening has served Vicar Lane well; it is still an important part of the public transport system and traffic still moves quite adequately in both directions – assisted of course with traffic lights, double yellow lines and bus lay-bys.

WELLINGTON STREET

The view is from City Square looking west along the southern side of Wellington Street where the height of the street has been constantly challenged. Wellington Chambers on the left in the old picture was triangular and extended on to both Aire Street and Wellington Street. From around 1910, Walter Bairstow's gents' hairdressing business occupied the corner premises, remaining there until 1980 when the building was demolished. Obviously, there was to be no room for this type of trader in City Square House built on the site in 1983 only to be demolished around 2005. Another triangular building also to be known as City Square House is currently in the development stage by the McAleer & Rushe Group. Designed by DLA Architecture Ltd, the building, when completed, is intended to reach 14 storeys high.

WELLINGTON STREET

Wellington Street once had several railway stations along its southern side. Leeds Central closed in 1967 and Royal Mail House was built on the site 1974/5. Closure came in 1998 and part of the building was converted and added to, becoming West Point in 2005 – a 65-metres-tall, 17-floor tower block seen completed on the right in the bottom picture. In front of West Point is the Wellington Plaza offices which replaced the Lancashire & Yorkshire Railway Goods offices. On the left in the top picture the Central Station pub, now the Central, has also been known over the years as Scruffy Murphy's and Wellington.

WESTGATE TUNNEL

Stage three of the Inner Relief Road, including the Westgate Tunnel, is seen under construction on 17 August 1973 in the top picture. The Tunnel was opened during February 1974 and this section of the Inner Relief Road in 1975. Commercial premises visible above the tunnel include those belonging to John Barran & Sons Ltd, Benjamin Simon & Sons; Marlbeck Fashions; and Centaur Clothing. The total cost of the Inner Relief Road, designed and supervised by the City of Leeds Engineers' Department, was £12,500,000 at 1970 prices and a 75% grant was received.

WOODHOUSE LANE/WADE LANE/MARK LANE

Above, looking from Woodhouse Lane, with Mark Lane to the left, and the Headrow, showing Schofield's store in the distance, to the right, no buildings survive today. The commercial premises in the mid-distance and the properties immediate right were demolished and the sites redeveloped in the Lewis development and the Headrow widening scheme. In the modern picture, an area out of view to the left has been occupied by the St John's Shopping Centre since 1985. The space immediately in front was converted to Dortmund Square during 1980, celebrating ten years of twinning with Dortmund.

YORK STREET, LOOKING TOWARDS QUARRY HILL

The view looks over to the city bus station on St Peters Street/York Street and Quarry Hill Flats in the distance. The bus station opened on August 31, 1938 and still survives but the flats have gone. Karl Marx-Hof's Red Vienna housing showpiece had impressed a Leeds delegation visiting the complex and the Quarry Hill flats were designed on similar lines. Built to the designs of R.A. Livett, between 1934-38, the 938 Leeds flats, covering 36 acres of land, contained seven- and eight-storey blocks, and were occupied by approx. 3,000 people. Disappointingly, the flats were demolished in 1978 following numerous problems concerning the steel frame, Garchey waste disposal system and ongoing social issues and vandalism.